Date: 5/7/21

World Book, Inc.
180 North LaSalle Street
Suite 900
Chicago, Illinois 60601
USA

For information about other "True or False?" titles, as well as other World Book print and digital publications, please go to www.worldbook.com.

For information about other World Book publications, call 1-800-WORLDBK (967-5325).

For information about sales to schools and libraries, call 1-800-975-3250 (United States) or 1-800-837-5365 (Canada).

Library of Congress Cataloging-in-Publication Data for this volume has been applied for.

True or False?
ISBN: 978-0-7166-4069-1 (set, hc.)

UFO'S
ISBN: 978-0-7166-4079-0 (hc.)

Also available as:
ISBN: 978-0-7166-4089-9 (e-book)

Printed in the United States of America by CG Book Printers, North Mankato, Minnesota

1st printing March 2020

Staff

Executive Committee

President
Geoff Broderick

Vice President, Finance
Donald D. Keller

Vice President, Marketing
Jean Lin

Vice President, International
Maksim Rutenberg

Vice President, Technology
Jason Dole

Director, Content and Product Development
Tom Evans

Director, Human Resources
Bev Ecker

Editorial

Writer
Madeline King

Manager, New Content Development
Jeff De La Rosa

Librarian
S. Thomas Richardson

Manager, Indexing Services
David Pofelski

Digital

Director, Digital Product Development
Erika Meller

Digital Product Manager
Jonathan Wills

Graphics and Design

Senior Designers
Don Di Sante
Isaiah Sheppard

Senior Visual Communications Designer
Melanie Bender

Media Editor
Rosalia Bledsoe

Manufacturing/Production

Manufacturing Manager
Anne Fritzinger

Production Specialist
Curley Hunter

Proofreader
Nathalie Strassheim

UFO'S

WORLD BOOK

www.worldbook.com

TRUE OR FALSE?

The letters *UFO* stand for *uncommon floating object.*

A UFO is an
unidentified flying object.
People sometimes call UFO's
flying saucers.

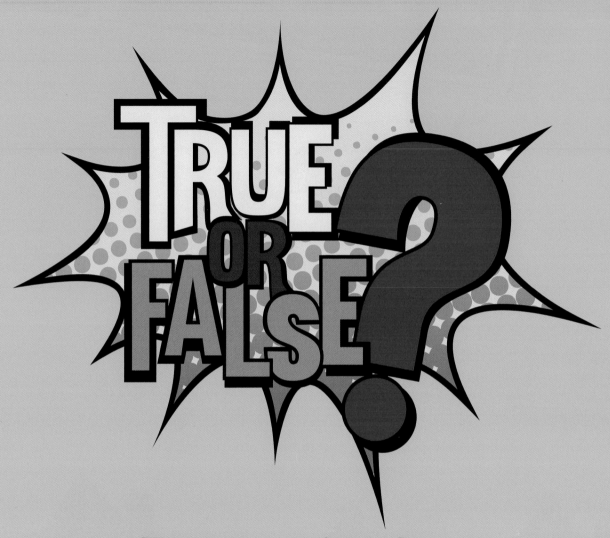

There are strict rules
for determining what is
considered a UFO.

The only rule is that the object is flying and that the observer cannot identify it.

People in the ancient world saw spaceships in the sky.

But they did think there were unusual things in the sky. Many of the objects that were strange to them were actually comets or meteors. To them, these objects fit the definition of a UFO.

Ancient peoples memorialized their UFO sightings on clothing.

17

But they did depict in their art and literature the unidentified objects they saw. Historians have found such depictions in art from the ancient Sumerians, Egyptians, Greeks, and Romans.

TRUE OR FALSE?

Some people believe UFO's come from other planets.

Many people think that UFO's are spaceships from other planets.

TRUE OR FALSE?

UFO's are sometimes called *flying saucers* because they shake off a sugary liquid that tastes like sweet tea.

But that would be delicious. In 1947, an airplane pilot named Kenneth Arnold saw several objects in the sky. He described them as moving like "a saucer if you skip it across water." But newspaper reporters muddled the description, saying the objects looked like flying saucers.

The study of UFO's is called *ufology.*

TRUE!

Some people, called *ufologists*, study UFO's for a living.

31

The best and brightest people who study ufology earn a gold medal when they see 51 UFO's. The medal is called "Area 51."

AREA 51

Area 51 is a United States military installation the Nevada desert. Many people think that scientists study UFO's at Area 51.

WARNING
AREA 51
Restricted Area

It is unlawful to enter this area without permission of the Installation Commander.
Sec.21, International Security Act of 1950; 50 U.S.C.797

While on this installation all personnel and the property under their control are subject to search.

USE OF DEADLY FORCE AUTHORIZED

AREA 51

Only people in the United States report seeing UFO's.

FALSE!

People all over the world have
reported seeing UFO's.

People have mistaken birds for UFO's.

40

TRUE!

Some people have also mistaken aircraft, insect swarms, and weather balloons for UFO's.

TRUE OR FALSE?

The planet Saturn has been mistaken for a UFO.

44

FALSE!

At least, not that anyone will admit. But, pilots have mistaken the planet Venus for a UFO many times.

46

McMinnville, Oregon, in the
United States, is known for its
UFO photos.

49

In 1950, photographs of a supposed UFO were taken from a farm near McMinnville. The sighting was published in *Life* magazine, making the town famous. The interest surrounding the photos led to an annual UFO festival.

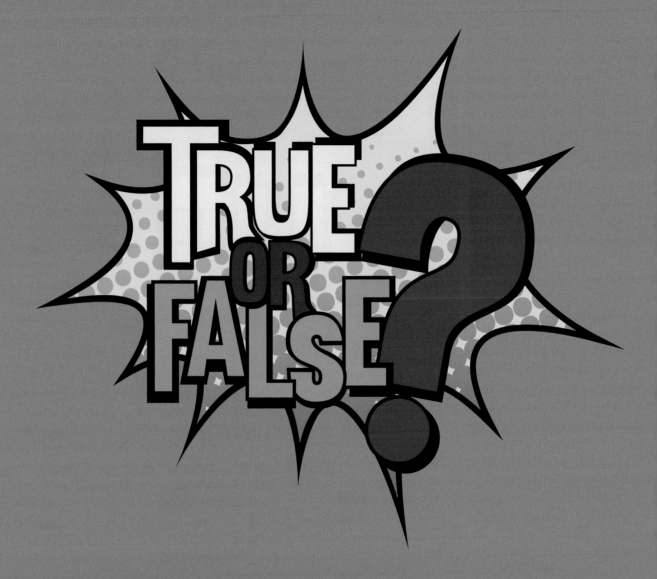

Project Blue Book is a blue book that contains a list of all the UFO sightings recorded.

FALSE!

Project Blue Book was a project by the United States Air Force to investigate UFO sightings. It concluded that one UFO sighting, in 1951, was probably caused by birds reflecting the light from street lamps.

TRUE OR FALSE?

UFO sightings always involve only one person or a small group of people.

Between 1989 and 1990, more than 13,000 people in Belgium reported seeing the same UFO. The string of sightings became known as the Belgian Wave.

58

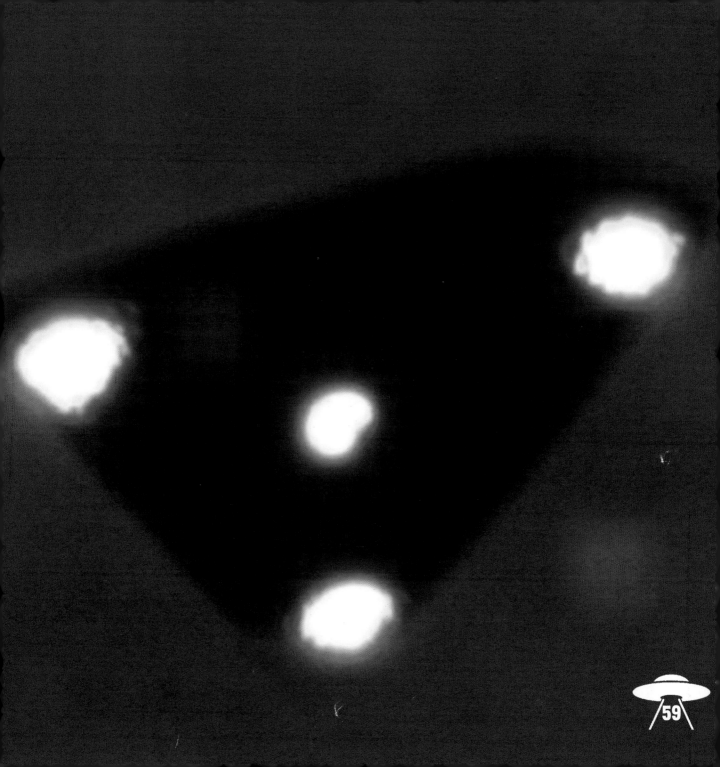

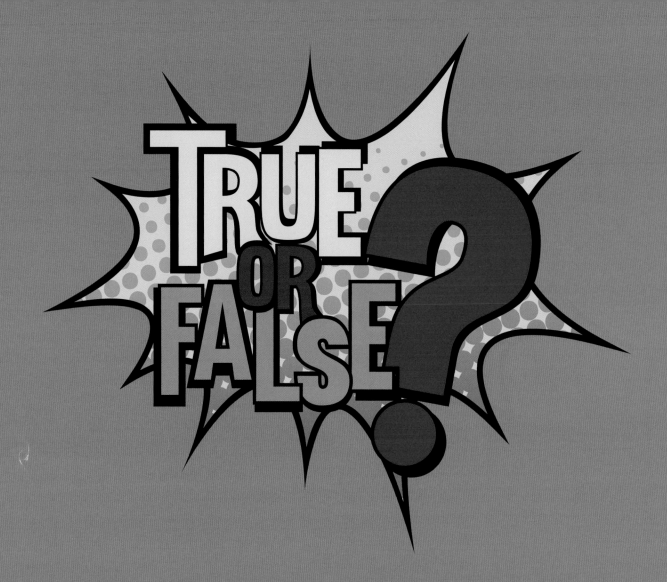

The South American nation of Brazil is the place to go if you want to see a UFO.

60

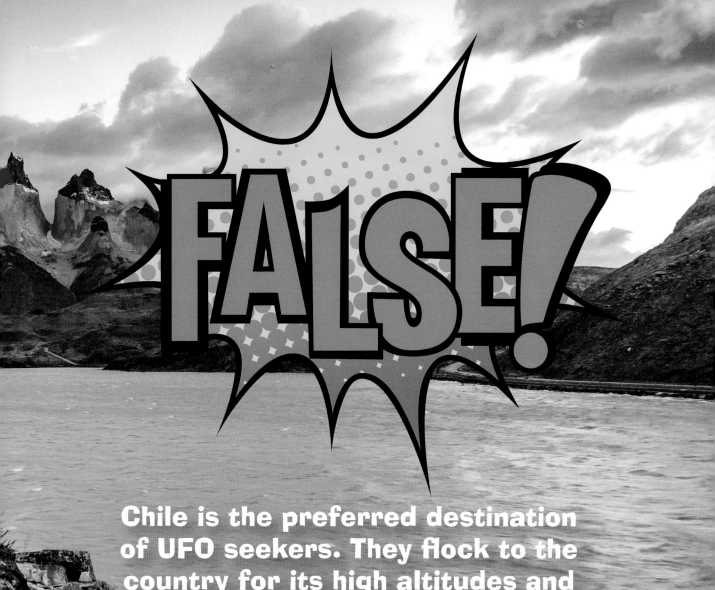

FALSE!

Chile is the preferred destination of UFO seekers. They flock to the country for its high altitudes and clear skies free of clouds and pollution.

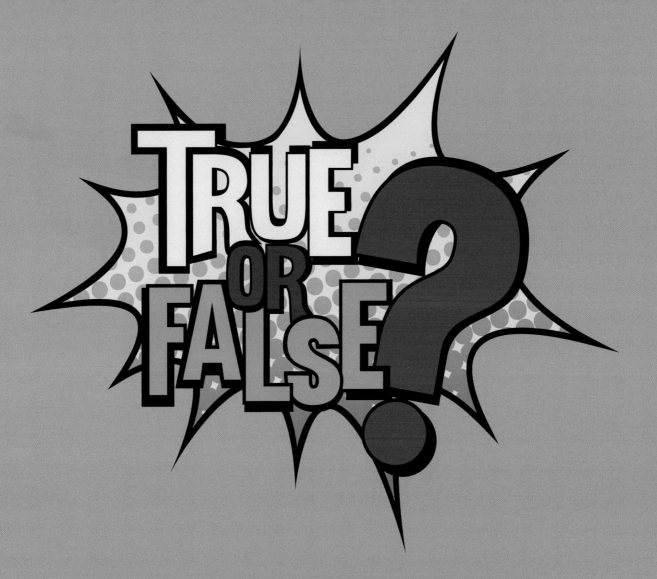

TRUE OR FALSE?

A *crop circle* is when you arrange all the vegetables on your plate in a circle.

FALSE!

A crop circle is circle or other shape formed in a field by the flattening of crops. Some people think crop circles are formed by UFO's.

68

UFO invasions have been popular in motion pictures since the 1950's.

69

Some early UFO invasion classics were
The Day the Earth Stood Still (1951) and
The War of the Worlds (1953).

A 1938 radio broadcast based on the novel *The War of the Worlds* (1898), by the English author H. G. Wells, left many listeners in a state of panic.

73

STAND BY
ON THE

CBS

CBS

14

TRUE!

The production, by the American actor and director Orson Welles, was so realistic that many listeners thought it was a news broadcast and that Martians were invading New Jersey, in the United States.

There is an organization dedicated to studying UFO's.

The organization, called the Center for UFO Studies, is headquartered in Chicago, Illinois, in the United States.

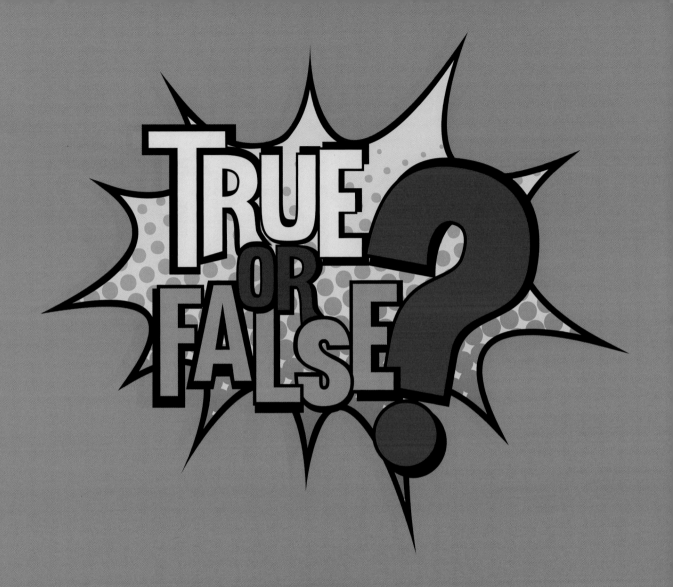

The most famous UFO crash allegedly occurred in Moscow, Russia.

Go nearly 6,000 miles (10,000 kilometers) east to Roswell, New Mexico, in the United States. In 1947, people claimed to find the wreckage of a spacecraft with alien pilots there. Skeptics think it was a weather balloon.

Leased Wire
Associated Press

RECORD PHONES
Business Office 2288
News Department 2287

5c PER COPY.

Roswell Daily Record

ROSWELL, NEW MEXICO, TUESDAY, JULY 8, 1947

VOL. 47, NUMBER 99. ESTABLISHED 1888

Movies as Usual

GRAND

Levees broke and flood waters rolled into the town of Grand Tower, Ill., but while the manager of the movie theater sweeps out the water that has entered the lobby these youngsters are standing in line for tickets for the night's performance. (AP Wirephoto).

Some of Soviet Satellites May Attend Paris Meeting

Paris, July 8 (AP)—Indications mounted today that at least some of the satellites within the Soviet world would attend the Marshall aid conference on the Marshall aid.

A Sofia dispatch quoted an authoritative source as saying Bulgaria would be represented at the Paris conference, which opens in Paris Saturday, which indicates that the Russian satellite states would be represented in the matter.

Despite a Moscow radio broadcast which had reported the Soviet-French invitation to participate, observers in Belgrade said the Yugoslavs still had not replied, and probably will not do so, following the advice of the Russians who had rejected the plan.

Roswellians Have Differing Opinions On Flying Saucers

Roswell is a not uncertain about how flying disks, it would appear from observations today with a number of local citizens, who have as many ideas concerning them.

Claims Army Is Stacking Courts Martial

Indiana Senator Lays Protest Before Patterson

Washington, July 8 (AP)—Contending that the Army stacks courts martial, Senator Jenner (R-Ind) commented today that the hub commanding the European theatre is blacking the courts against the defendants in court martial.

In a letter to Secretary of War Patterson demanding a halt the investigation of army military that proceedings, Jenner charged that he said was unnecessary demands.

House Passes Tax Slash by Large Margin

Defeat Amendment By Demos to Remove Many from Rolls

Washington, July 8 (AP)—The house passed today the Republican-backed bill to cut income taxes 14,000,000,000 across the board for 40,000,000 taxpayers, beginning Jan. 1.

Security Council Paves Way to Talks On Arms Reductions

Lake Success, July 8 (AP)—The United Nations security council today approved an American blueprint for arms reduction despite the plan that would bettle school efforts.

The vote was 9 to 0, with Russia and Poland abstaining.

No Details of Flying Disk Are Revealed

Roswell Hardware Man and Wife Report Disk Seen

The Intelligence office of the 509th Bombardment group at Roswell Army Air Field announced at noon today, that the field has come into possession of a flying

Ex-King Carol Weds Mme. Lupescu

Former King Carol of Romania and Mme. Elena Lupescu relax aboard the S. S. America bound for Cuba and Mexico in May, 1941. A member of Carol's household in Rio de Janeiro said the ex-king and his companion for 23 years in reign and exile were recently married at their hotel. Copacabana Palace suite. (AP Wirephoto).

Miners and Operators Sign Highest Wage Pact in History

Washington, July 8 (AP)—An agreement granting a million soft coal miners the highest wage rate in history was signed today by John L. Lewis and the operators.

American League Wins All-Star Game

Chicago, July 8 (AP)—The American league, pecking away with an eight hit attack and singling in at least two runs.

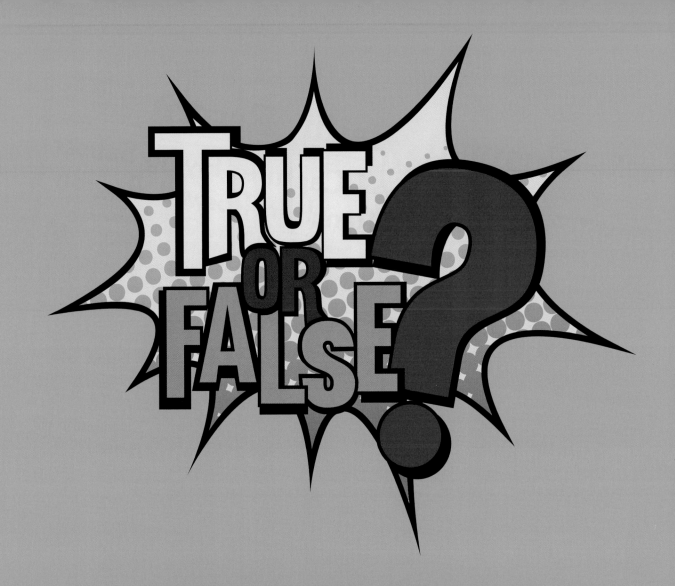

UFO's kidnap people.

Many people claim to have been abducted
by aliens in UFO's. But no such claims have
ever been proven.

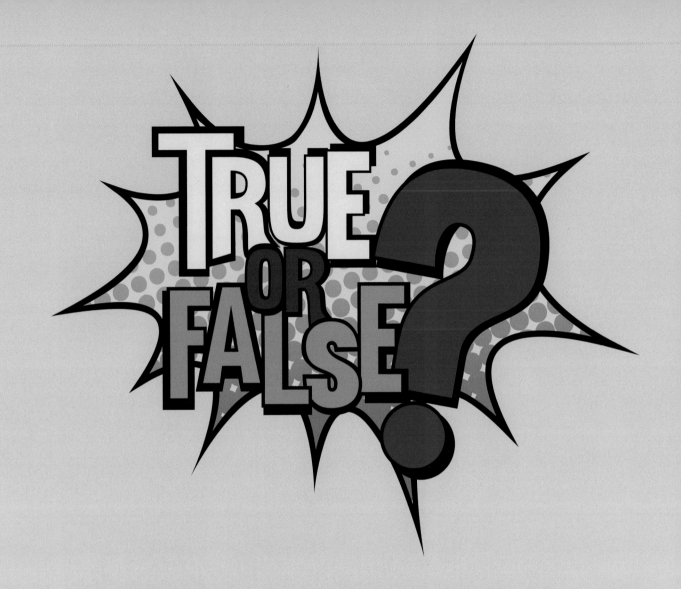

You can be fined for making up
a UFO sighting.

**Two men in New Jersey in the
United States were fined $250
for using fire and fishing lines to
stage a UFO *hoax* (trick or prank).**

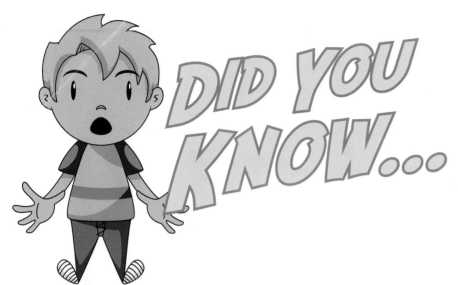

DID YOU KNOW...

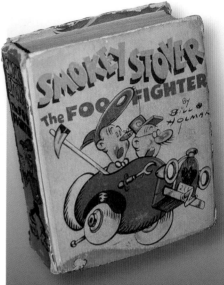

A supposed UFO appeared in **an image of the sun** taken by the National Aeronautics and Space Administration (NASA). The cause turned out to be a problem with the camera.

A cartoon inspired another name for UFO's: **foo fighters.** Smokey Stover would say, "Where there's foo, there's fire." Airmen saw lights in the sky and named them foo fighters.

Some people think a condition called *sleep paralysis* is responsible for reports of

UFO abductions.

A person with sleep paralysis briefly cannot move and may feel as if being watched—possibly by aliens.

The American ufologist J. Allen Hynek coined the term *close encounter* for a

UFO sighting

at a distance of less than 500 feet (150 meters).

A **droplet of water** on an airplane window was mistaken for a UFO.

Index

Acknowledgments

Cover: © Alex F, Shutterstock; © Mochipet/Shutterstock;
         © Filborg/Shutterstock
4-25   © Shutterstock
26   U.S. Air Force
29-42   © Shutterstock
45   © Mark Garlick, Science Photo Library/Getty Images
46-47   © Diana Robinson Photography/Getty Images
48-49   © Bettmann/Getty Images
50-56   © Shutterstock
59   Public Domain
61-70   © Shutterstock
73   Public Domain
74   © Universal History Archive/Getty Images
77   ©Tom Kelley Archive/Getty Images
78-79   © Marchello74/Shutterstock; © CUFOS
80-93   © Shutterstock

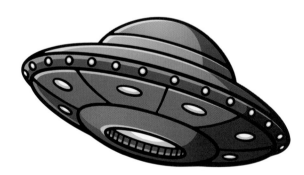